No Time For Christmas

D1511286

Created by Valerie Howard

Cast of Characters:

PJ McIntyre: older boy or girl (22 lines)

Rebecca McIntyre: younger girl (13 lines)

Mrs. McIntyre: adult or older teen (6 lines)

Miss Baldwin: adult or older teen (16 lines)

Daniel: funny, older boy (11 lines)

Lucy: take-charge, older girl (11 lines)

Chrissy: cute little girl (4 lines)

Kid #1 (3 lines)

Kid #2 (2 lines)

Kid #3 (2 lines)

Scene I

At practice on stage. Kids stand on risers to sing, then gather in front of them to talk after song is done. All characters but PJ and Rebecca are on the risers .
Curtains open.
Lights up.
Sing Go Tell it on the Mountain.

Go Tell it on the Mountain
by John W. Work II

Chorus:
Go, tell it on the mountain,
Over the hills and everywhere.
Go, tell it on the mountain
That Jesus Christ is born.

While shepherds kept their watching
O'er silent flocks by night,
Behold, throughout the heavens
There shone a holy light.
Chorus

The shepherds feared and trembled
When lo, above the earth
Rang out the angel chorus
That hailed our Savior's birth!
Chorus

Down in a lonely manger
The humble Christ was born
And God sent us salvation
That blessed Christmas morn.
Chorus

PJ and Rebecca come in halfway through the song and join the other kids on the risers. They are obviously late, but their entrance shouldn't distract the audience from the song's message.

Miss Baldwin *(clapping)*: Beautifully done, children. *(Looks at watch.)* And that wraps practice up for today. May I encourage all of you to be punctual to our caroling outing tomorrow afternoon?

The other kids glance at PJ and Rebecca, they nod and look sheepish.

PJ: Yes, Miss Baldwin.

Miss Baldwin *(picking up a clipboard and waving it)*: I also have some blank spaces left on this sign up sheet. Our Christmas concert is in one week, and we need everyone pitching in to help with set up, decorations, refreshments, and clean up. *(Sets clipboard down on a stool, desk, or small stand.)* See you tomorrow.

Miss Baldwin exits.

PJ, Rebecca, Daniel, Chrissy, Lucy, and Kid #1 gather around the clipboard, Lucy picks it up and studies it.

Daniel: Why were you and Rebecca so late to practice today, PJ?

PJ *(shrugs)*: Mom thought choir practice started at six and the bake sale at school started at five. But really choir practice started at five and the bake sale isn't until next Friday. Traffic was moving so slow, it took us thirty minutes to drive across town. We'll be on time tomorrow.

Lucy: Okay, it looks like we need three more people to sign up to bring desserts, someone to hang the Christmas lights, someone to help set up, and someone to help clean up.

Kid #1: I'll bring some brownies. *(Lucy writes a name down.)*

Daniel: Put me down for hanging the lights, that sounds easy. *(Lucy writes his name down.)*

Lucy *(with a yawn)*: I'll help set up since I'll be here early anyway. My dad is running the sound system and he'll have to check all the microphones and speakers before the concert. *(Writes her name.)* PJ, what do you and Rebecca want to do?

PJ: I guess Rebecca and Mom can make another gingerbread house. They already have to make two more for the bake sale since the ones they made for today will be long gone next week. And I'll help with clean up duty. *(Lucy marks more names on the sheet and puts the clipboard down.)*

Lucy: Okay, that about does it. I've got to run home to finish up the big science project for Mrs. Flinn's class. It's due on Monday. Bye!

All Other Kids *(waving and dispersing off-stage)*: Bye! Me too! See you later! Have fun with that! (etc.)

Close curtain.
Lights fade.

Scene II

PJ and Rebecca's house. PJ is sitting in a chair or at a desk/table with a textbook, reading. Rebecca is standing next to him tapping his shoulder when curtain opens.

Curtain opens.
Lights up.

PJ *(swatting at Rebecca's hand)*: Rebecca, I told you, I have to read this chapter for school tomorrow. Now, please leave me alone.

Rebecca: But I want to ask you a question.

PJ: Not right now. I need to read this before Mom takes us to go caroling. I won't have time to get it done later. You're lucky that your teachers don't assign homework on weekends, but you really need to go away and let me get this done!

Rebecca: Why did you wait until Sunday to do your homework, anyway?

PJ: I didn't have time before now. I need to get this done, so please go away.

Rebecca *(whining and stomping foot)*: But, it's important.

PJ: I'm sure it's an extremely important question, like, "Do unicorns have purple hair?" or "What do bunnies dream about?" But I'm telling you, seriously, ask me later.

Mrs. McIntyre enters.

Mrs. McIntyre: Rebecca, let PJ finish his homework, please.

PJ: Thank you!

Rebecca *(turning to mom)*: Well can I ask you my question then?

Mrs. McIntyre: Let me ask one first. Who decided I needed to make a gingerbread house for the church's Christmas concert?

(PJ hides his face behind his book, Rebecca points to him.)

Mrs. McIntyre: PJ?

PJ *(acting innocent)*: Huh? What?

Mrs. McIntyre: If you think the concert needs a gingerbread house, then I guess you can be the one to help me make it.

PJ: Yes, Mom.

Rebecca: Now can I ask my question?

Mrs. McIntyre: Oh, Sweetie, can it wait? Right now you need to come help me pack the cookies for Mrs. Green's cookie swap tonight.

PJ *(slamming the book closed)*: Done!

Mrs. McIntyre: Good, now you can help us pack cookies before you get ready for caroling. Let's get a move on.

McIntyres exit.
Lights fade.
Curtain closes.

Scene III

Outside the shopping center. Lucy and Kid #2 are holding flyers and Chrissy has a big bucket labeled "Donations". The rest of the kids are on the risers. Curtain opens. Lights up. Sing O Come All Ye Faithful.

O Come All Ye Faithful
by John Francis Wade

O come all ye faithful,
Joyful and triumphant,
O come ye, O come ye to Bethlehem!
Come and behold Him,
Born the King of angels!

Chorus:
O come, let us adore Him,
O come, let us adore Him,
O come, let us adore Him,
Christ the Lord!

Sing choirs of angels,
Sing in exultation,
O sing, all ye bright hosts of heav'n above!
Glory to God, all glory in the highest!
Chorus

Yea, Lord, we greet Thee,
Born this happy morning,
Jesus, to Thee be all glory given;
Word of the Father, now in flesh appearing!
Chorus

Miss Baldwin: Great job, kids! I know it's cold out here. I'm going to run to my car and get the hot chocolate. I'll be right back. Lucy and PJ, you're both in charge until I get back.

Miss Baldwin exits.

Lucy *(frustrated)*: One flyer! I've only handed out one flyer in two hours! And the guy who took it just spit his gum in it and crumpled it up!

Kid #2 *(with stack of flyers in hand)*: Some woman almost walked right into me because she was staring at her cell phone. Didn't even apologize.

Daniel: This is a waste of time. Everyone around here has something better to do than stop and listen to us sing. I should be home trying to untangle that mess of Christmas lights Miss Baldwin gave me.

PJ: Maybe we just need to sing louder.

Rebecca *(shivering)*: I'm so c-c-cold. Can we go home?

Chrissy *(holding the donations bucket and an apple core or other piece of trash)*: What do you want me to do with this? Someone thought our bucket was a trash can because they didn't stop to read it.

Lucy: Just go throw it away, Chrissy. Other than that, how much was donated?

Chrissy *(looking down into the bucket)*: A quarter, two dimes, and a penny.

Kid #3: That's all?

Kid #1: This is impossible!

PJ: Look at this parking lot. Crammed full of people running from one store to the next getting ready for Christmas, and they can't even stop for a second to take a flyer or donate to a worthy cause.

Kids looking out to the "parking lot" shaking their heads in disbelief when Miss Baldwin returns with a large insulated container and foam cups.

Miss Baldwin: I have hot cocoa, everyone! Take a seat where you are and I'll pass it out. Now, raise your hand if you want some.

A few children raise their hands, including Rebecca. Everyone is looking gloomy and defeated. Miss Baldwin passes out cups to the kids who raised their hands and mimes pouring hot chocolate during the following dialogue.

Miss Baldwin: What's the matter? Aren't you having fun?

Kid # 2: No one will take our flyers.

Chrissy: And people think I'm collecting trash.

Rebecca: And it's so c-c-cold!

Daniel: Maybe we should just call it a day, Miss Baldwin. No one wants us here.

Other kids nod and vocalize their agreement.

Miss Baldwin *(looking thoughtful)*: Well, I'm sorry it's been such a rough day, but you need to remember what we're here for. We're not just here to hand out flyers or collect money. We're not just here so people will congratulate us on our singing abilities or agree to come to our concert on Saturday.

Lucy *(shocked)*: We're not?

Miss Baldwin: No, not primarily. We're here to remind people of the true meaning of Christmas. So, let's put a smile on our faces, stand up, and see how much energy we can put in our next song.

Kids reluctantly put their hot cocoa mugs down and stand up, trying to smile and look energetic. Sing O Little Town of Bethlehem

O Little Town of Bethlehem
by Phillips Brooks

O little town of Bethlehem,
How still we see thee lie!
Above thy deep and dreamless sleep
The silent stars go by.
Yet in thy dark streets shineth
The everlasting Light;
The hopes and fears of all the years
Are met in thee tonight.

For Christ is born of Mary,
And gathered all above,
While mortals sleep, the angels keep
Their watch of wond'ring love.
O morning stars, together,
Proclaim the holy birth!
And praises sing to God the King,
And peace to men on earth.

How silently, how silently,
The wondrous gift is giv'n!
So God imparts to human hearts
The blessings of His heav'n.
No ear may hear His coming,
But in this world of sin,
Where meek souls will receive Him, still
The dear Christ enters in.

O holy Child of Bethlehem!
Descend to us, we pray;
Cast out our sin, and enter in;
Be born in us today.
We hear the Christmas angels
The great glad tidings tell;
O come to us, abide with us,
Our Lord Emmanuel!

Miss Baldwin: Good job. And look, Lucy, you passed out two more flyers, and Chrissy, you collected some more donations. Now, I want to see everyone on time to our last practice on Friday night. You are dismissed.

Children filter off the risers and off stage, still looking a little upset.

Lights fade.
Curtain closes.

Scene IV

Everyone in practice room scurrying around, running here and there, handling papers, clipboards, decorating a tree, untangling lights, etc. Daniel has a string of white Christmas lights wrapped around his torso (not lit up), looking frazzled.

Curtain opens.
Lights up.

Miss Baldwin: Quickly, everyone, quickly! The concert is tomorrow! Get those decorations on the tree! Get those lights up, Daniel. *(Grabs the sign-up clipboard.)* No one is bringing Christmas cookies? How can we have a Christmas concert without Christmas cookies? *(Looks around frantically, but no one is stopping what they're doing.)* I guess I can make some tomorrow morning. *(Sighs and signs her name to the list.)*

Lucy *(searching everywhere)*: Where's the decoration box?

PJ *(pointing to the box)*: I think I saw it over there. *(Lucy finds it and kneels next to it, starts pulling decorations out.)*

Daniel *(walking across stage counting light bulbs on the string of lights)*: 746, good, 747, good, 748, good...

Two kids (can be Kid #1 and Kid #2) start playing tug-of-war with a string of garland.

Miss Baldwin: Garland is not for tug-of-war, you two. Stop fooling around and put it on the tree now, please. *(Kids obey.)*

Kid #3 *(holding an ornament and reaching toward the top of the Christmas tree)*: I can't reach!

Miss Baldwin comes and takes the ornament from Kid #3 and hangs it on the tree herself, then collapses into a nearby chair.

Miss Baldwin: Okay, everyone, it's almost time to go. I can finish up tomorrow afternoon. Put everything away and gather over here. We only have time to practice one last song today. Turn to page 16 in your songbooks.

Kids put decorations in the box and gather on risers. They grab their books and open them.

Miss Baldwin: One, Two, Three..

Sing God Rest Ye Merry Gentlemen.

God Rest Ye Merry Gentlemen
by Unknown Author

God rest ye merry, gentlemen.
Let nothing you dismay.
Remember, Christ, our Savior
Was born on Christmas day!
To save us all from Satan's power
When we were gone astray.

Chorus:
O tidings of comfort and joy,
Comfort and joy.
O tidings of comfort and joy.

From God our Heavenly Father
A blessed angel came;
And unto certain shepherds
Brought tidings of the same:
How that in Bethlehem was born
The Son of God by name.
Chorus

And when they came to Bethlehem
Where our dear Savior lay,
They found Him in a manger,
Where oxen feed on hay;
His mother Mary kneeling down,
Unto the Lord did pray.
Chorus

Now to the Lord sing praises,
All you within this place,
And with true love and brotherhood
Each other now embrace;
This holy tide of Christmas
All other doth deface.
Chorus

Miss Baldwin: Wonderful! I think we're finally ready for the concert. Everyone go home and get a good night's sleep. I want to see you here on time and smiling tomorrow night!

Everyone exits as lights fade.
Curtain closes.

Scene V

Curtain opens.
Lights up.
Miss Baldwin enters and walks to center stage.

Miss Baldwin: Thank you all for taking the time to come out to our church's 31st annual children's Christmas concert. I hope you all enjoy the decorations, the singing, and the lovely refreshments that the children and their parents worked so hard to put together for you this evening.

Children enter and get on risers. Miss Baldwin turns to kids to direct them. Music starts the intro. Kids all take a deep breath to start singing. Music and lights are cut abruptly to simulate a power outage. Kids gasp.

Miss Baldwin: PJ, can you go get some candles in the decoration box please? Ladies and gentlemen, please remain calm and in your seats, and our Christmas concert will continue momentarily. Boys and girls, I'm going to go find out what's going on. Just sit tight and PJ will get you some candles. Thank you.

Kids sit on risers. PJ passes out flameless candles to children enough to light the cast member's faces. PJ sits with other children. Miss Baldwin exits.

Lucy: This is a catastrophe! After all our hard work, everything is ruined! It's not fair!

Daniel: I think I'm going to cry.

PJ: We can still sing by candlelight, Daniel, it will be okay.

Daniel: I'm not worried about the singing. It's just...no one will be able to see all the lights I put up. Do you know how long that took me? First I spend three hours untangling them. Three hours! Then I plugged them in and they didn't work. I had to check every light bulb until I found the broken one. It was the last bulb on the string of a thousand. One thousand!

Kid #1: I guess you should have started checking on the other end.

Daniel *(frustrated)*: I know!

Chrissy: Lucy? I'm scared of the dark.

Lucy: It's okay, Chrissy. Miss Baldwin is trying to get the lights back on. Here, hold this candle, it's really bright.

Rebecca: Pssst! PJ? Can I ask you my question now?

PJ: Now?

Rebecca: Yeah.

PJ *(sighing)*: I guess so, it's not like I'm doing anything else at the moment. What's your question?

Rebecca: My question is: why do we have to celebrate Christmas when it just makes everyone crazy?

PJ: What? Why do you think Christmas makes people crazy?

Rebecca: Well, you've been ignoring me. Lucy was mad that she only handed out three flyers on Sunday. And all those people in the parking lot looked extra grumpy. And Miss Baldwin almost fainted at practice last night.

Daniel *(still moaning)*: One thousand light bulbs. One thousand light bulbs!

Rebecca *(holds her hand out, palm up, to indicate Daniel as if to say "see?" or "case in point")*: And I heard Mom tell Mrs. Green that she couldn't wait for Christmas to be over so everything can go back to normal. Why do we bother with Christmas when all it does is make people crazy?

Lucy: She's got a point, PJ. Look how stressed everyone's been over this one concert.

PJ: I know. You're right, Rebecca. The Christmas activities got a little out of control this year. Miss Baldwin said it best when we were caroling: the important thing is that we remember the real reason for Christmas.

Rebecca: Presents?

PJ: No, not presents. Christmas isn't about the presents, the decorations, the gingerbread houses, the craft fairs, the concerts, or the lights.

Daniel *(moaning)*: Oh, the lights!

PJ: It's a time to remember the very first Christmas– when God sent His Son, Jesus, to be born in a dirty barn and grow up to be the Savior that would die for our sins. If we don't take time to think about that, then I guess we haven't truly celebrated Christmas at all.

Lucy: I guess I haven't been really celebrating Christmas, then.

Daniel: Me either.

PJ: But we can start. Whether this concert happens or not, whether people appreciate our decorations and refreshments or not, I'm going to remember the first Christmas and stop making myself crazy with all the distractions. I'm going to remember that Jesus was born to die for my sins, and I'm going to celebrate the real reason for the season.

Lights up.
Miss Baldwin reenters.

Miss Baldwin: Thank you for your patience, folks. Seems we blew a fuse with all the extra lights plugged in, but the issue has been resolved and we can begin! *(Turning to the children.)* One, two, three!

Sing The First Noel.

The First Noel
by Unknown Author

The first Noel, the angel did say,
Was to certain poor shepherds in fields as they lay:
In fields where they lay keeping their sheep,
On a cold winter's night that was so deep.

Chorus:
Noel, Noel, Noel, Noel,
Born is the King of Israel.

They looked up and saw a star
Shining in the east, beyond them far,
And to the earth it gave great light,
And so it continued both day and night.
Chorus

And by the light of that same star
Three wise men came from country far;
To seek for a King was their intent,
And to follow the star wherever it went.
Chorus

This star drew nigh to the north-west,
O'er Bethlehem it took its rest,
And there it did both stop and stay,
Right over the place where Jesus lay.
Chorus

Then entered in those wise men three,
Fell reverently upon their knee,
And offered there in His presence
Their gold, and myrrh, and frankincense.
Chorus

Then let us all with one accord
Sing praises to our heavenly Lord,
That hath made heav'n and earth of naught,
And with His blood mankind hath bought.
Chorus

Everyone bows.
Lights fade.
Curtain closes.

Props:

Risers
Stool or small table
Clipboard
Pen
Textbook
Chair and desk or table
Flyers or stacks of colorful paper
Bucket labeled with the word "Donations"
Apple core or similar trash item
Large Thermos
Foam cups
Box of Christmas decorations
Christmas ornaments
String of garland
Christmas tree
Several strings of Christmas lights
Songbooks
Flameless candles

Costumes:

Scenes I, II, and IV:

Kids wearing casual, inside "Saturday" attire. (Jeans, T-shirts, sweatshirts, etc.)

Scene III:

Kids wearing outerwear like mittens, hats, boots and scarves.

Scene V:

Kids wearing choir robes or dressed up for concert.

Transition from Scene IV to V suggestions:

If your church doesn't have choir robes for the kids to slip on over their clothes for the concert, the girls can slip long skirts on over their weekend pants/jeans and wear the same plain colored shirts as they've been wearing throughout the play. Boys can have button-up dress shirts on under zip-up sweatshirts or put nice sweaters on over their casual weekend T-shirts to become more "dressed up" for the concert.

Variations:

The music teacher character can be played by a man. The new character would simply be named Mr. Baldwin.

For fewer cast members:

Mrs. McIntyre's lines can be called out from off-stage by Miss Baldwin.

Kid #1, Kid #2, and Kid #3's lines can be combined and spoken by one character.

If you enjoyed this play, you might also like ...

Christmas Lights by Valerie Howard

Christmas Gifts by Valerie Howard

Christmas Catastrophe by Steve and Valerie Howard

The Worst Christmas Ever by Elizabeth Rowe and Juliet Rowe

Find books for children, teens, and adults at
www.AuthorValerieHoward.com

Follow what's new at
www.Facebook.com/ValerieHowardBooks

Made in the USA
Middletown, DE
10 October 2022

12443431R00015